D1310520

It's Crazy How Much I Love That You're My Sister

FROM: _____

TO: _____

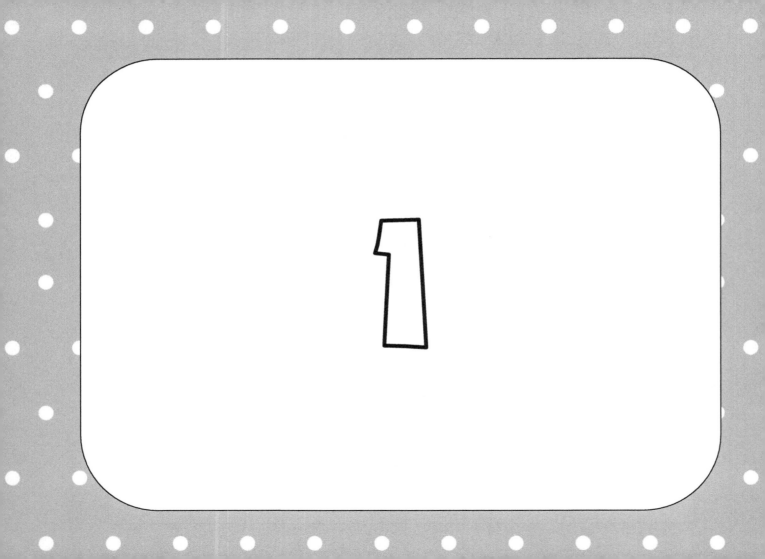

I love that we're

_____

_____

_____

I love you because
you have a nice

_____

_____

_____

you have an awesome

_____

_____

_____

You deserve to

_____

_____

_____

The funniest thing you do is

_____

_____

_____

The best thing about you is

_____

_____

_____

You are such a good

_____

_____

_____

My favorite adventure with you has been

_____

_____

_____

I love your crazy way of

_____

_____

_____

Thank you for teaching me how to

_____

_____

I love that we have the same

_____

_____

_____

I love you because
you have an amazing

_____

_____

_____

You are better than a

_____

_____

_____

I was very proud of you when

_____

_____

_____

15

I love when we

_____

_____

together

You are good at

_____

_____

_____

I wish you

_____

_____

_____

in your life

I love how you inspire me to

_____

_____

_____

The best things I learned from you is

_____

_____

_____

20

You make me laugh
when you

_____

_____

_____

21

One quirky thing about you I love is

_____

_____

_____

22

You are there for me when

_____

_____

23

I don't like it when you

_____

_____

but

_____

_____

24

I love it when we

_____

_____

_____

25

I love that you're my sis, because of all that and because you have a great

_____

_____

_____

Made in United States
North Haven, CT
05 May 2022

18832919R00030